Nicolas
Bentley

The Prion Cartoon Classics series, brings together anthologies of drawings from the top artists in the field working in Britain and around the world. Concentrating on simple joke cartoons, the collections – which often bring an artist's work together in a single volume for the very first time – also contain brief biographies of each cartoonist. This unique series will be welcomed both by those who have long sought out-of-print books by the greatest cartoonists of the twentieth century, and also by those who simply want to enjoy the very best in visual humour.

Other Titles in the Prion Cartoon Classics Series
H.M.Bateman
David Langdon (forthcoming)
Leslie Starke (forthcoming)

Nicolas Bentley

Edited by Mark Bryant

PRION

First published in the UK in 2002 by
Prion Books Limited, Imperial Works,
Perren Street, London NW5 3ED

Collection and Introduction copyright © Mark Bryant 2002
Foreword copyright © Richard Ingrams 2002
All cartoons and drawings copyright © Bella Jones
and the Estate of Nicolas Bentley

ISBN 1-85375-459-5

Printed and bound in China
by Everbest Printing Co. Ltd

Foreword

by Richard Ingrams

I am delighted that Nicolas Bentley's cartoons are being published by Prion Books.

I knew Nick in two capacities. As an editor at André Deutsch he saw my first book, *God's Apology* (1977) to press. He also, for many years until his sad death, illustrated 'Auberon Waugh's Diary' in *Private Eye*. Bron and I were delighted to have this link with the world of Belloc and Chesterton. In both roles Nick was quiet, very meticulous and highly professional. Although he was himself an old-fashioned Leftie, he never objected to often outrageous ideas for illustrations.

As proof of his generosity he gave me all the drawings he did for a 'Beachcomber' collection I edited in 1974. Quiet, kind and generous, Nick had a very sharp eye. I remember John Betjeman telling me 'For such a nice person he is very good at drawing especially horrible people.'

Richard Ingrams

Contents

Editor's Note

Though made in consultation with Bentley's family this is very much a personal selection of his work. For maximum quality of reproduction only his black-and-white line drawings have been used. These have largely been taken from the three main cartoon anthologies which were published in his lifetime – *Die? I Thought I'd Laugh!* (1936), *Animal Vegetable and South Kensington* (1940) and *How Can you Bear to be Human?*(1957) – thereby ensuring that Bentley himself would have approved of them. However, I have also included a number of topical cartoons from the *Daily Mail* and other sources where the jokes are still relevant today and need little or no explanation, but have generally omitted his wartime cartoons as detailed historical and biographical background would be required to give them the full impact they deserve.

For help in the preparation of this book I greatly indebted to Bentley's daughter Bella Jones and her husband John for their constant encouragement and support and the loan of material – including a number of Bentley's *Daily Mail* cartoons which are reproduced here in book form for the first time. Thanks also go to Ruari McLean CBE, whose own book, *Nicolas Bentley Drew the Pictures* (1990) – now sadly out of print – has been a source of much inspiration. In addition my thanks go to Richard Ingrams for agreeing to write the Foreword. And last, but by no means least, many thanks to Barry Winkleman and Jim Pope of Prion Books for producing such a handsome book.

M.B.

Introduction

Nicolas Bentley FSIA FRSA (1907-78) was a man of many parts – book publisher, circus clown, film extra, novelist, mimic, journalist, script editor, Dickens scholar, fireman, poet, advertising man and commercial artist. The son of a journalist, his godfather was G.K. Chesterton and he soon built a formidable reputation as an illustrator. Among the 70-odd books which still carry the famous by-line 'Nicolas Bentley Drew the Pictures' are works by George Mikes, Hilaire Belloc, J.B. Morton, Damon Runyon, the Duke of Bedford, Lawrence Durrell, Kingsley Amis, E.M. Delafield and, perhaps most famously, T.S. Eliot's *Old Possum's Book of Practical Cats* – on which the hugely successful Andrew Lloyd-Webber musical *Cats* is based. However, he was also an extremely distinguished cartoonist and caricaturist and drew for most of the leading humorous publications of his day.

Born Nicholas Clerihew Bentley in Lymington Road, West Hampstead, London, on 14 June 1907, he was the youngest child of Edmund Clerihew Bentley (1875-1956). His father was the inventor of the 'clerihew' (Clerihew was Edmund's mother's maiden name) and author of one of the earliest detective novels, the bestselling *Trent's Last Case* (1913), among other books. In addition he was Deputy Editor of the *Daily News*, leader writer for the *Daily Telegraph* (1912-34) and an amateur artist who had been at school with G.K. Chesterton and at Oxford with John Buchan and Lord Birkenhead. Nicolas' mother was Violet Alice Mary Boileau (d.1949), daughter of General Neil Edmonstone Boileau of the Bengal Staff Corps in the Indian Army – whose aide-de-camp had once been Lord Roberts – and a descendant of the famous French poet and critic Nicolas Boileau (1636-1711). He was also a relative of Charles Dickens' friend Richard Bentley (1794-1871), the publisher of *Bentley's Miscellany* (edited by Dickens). His two elder siblings were Neil (who became an aeronautical engineer) and Betty (who died aged 18).

Educated at first at a Parents' National Educational Union school in Belsize Park, at the age of eight Bentley attended University College School, Hampstead. He then studied illustration at Heatherley's School of Art in London for 18 months (1924-25) – where a fellow student was Evelyn Waugh – and then worked very briefly as an (unpaid) clown for Ginnett's Circus in Wembley and as a film extra (1925). Just before the General Strike in 1926 he got a job as a studio assistant in the W. S. Crawford advertising agency whose artists included Edward McKnight Kauffer and Horace Taylor. The same year he sold his first drawing (to G.K. Chesterton). He later left Crawfords and from 1927 to 1928 worked in the studio of his former colleague the poster artist Horace Taylor in Church Row, Hampstead, before setting up his own studio in Kensington. Then followed a brief period selling advertising space on the financial pages on his father's paper, the *Daily Telegraph*. He received his first commercial commission to illustrate a diary in the monthly trade paper *Man and His Clothes* (January 1927 to December 1929) and in 1929 he drew the jacket for and contributed 11 drawings to *More Biography*, the second collection of his father's clerihews. The same year he illustrated his first book, *New Cautionary Tales* by Hilaire Belloc (another friend of his father).

In 1930 Bentley joined Shell-Mex's publicity office as personal assistant to its director, Jack Beddington, who had seen some of Bentley's work at a student exhibition at Heatherley's, and became part of the team that produced the celebrated 'Shell Guides' series. Artists and writers already working for Shell at the time included Edward Ardizzone, Rex Whistler and John Betjeman, and Bentley subsequently employed the cartoonists Walter Goetz and John Reynolds (illustrator of *1066 and All That*).

He left Shell-Mex in 1932 to become a freelance illustrator and commercial artist, producing humorous advertisements for Eno's Fruit Salt, Pan Yan Pickle, Sankey-Sheldon Steel and others. He also contributed cartoons to the *Bystander* (more than 100 cartoons from 1933 to 1940 when it was incorporated in the

Tatler), *Strand, Night & Day* (1937), *Radio Times, Good Housekeeping, Homes & Gardens* and *Punch* (from January 1933 to 1959) as well as *Lilliput* (cartoons and illustrations from its first issue, July 1937, until it merged with *Men Only* in August 1960) and *Men Only* (from its beginning in December 1935 until 1937). In addition he drew for the *Daily Express, Sunday Express, Daily Graphic, Sunday Graphic* and *Sunday Referee*. In 1932 he also illustrated another book *All Fall Down!* with texts by his father, Chesterton, J.B. Morton and others.

In October 1934 Bentley married the children's author Barbara Hastings, daughter of the celebrated barrister Sir Patrick Gardiner Hastings QC, who had been MP for Wallsend and Attorney-General in Ramsay MacDonald's first

'Now, sonny, I wouldn't cry that way.'
'Cry as you blooming well please – this is my way!'

Bentley's first drawing for *Punch*, published on 4 January 1933.

xi

Labour government in 1924. (Their only child Bella [Arabella] was born in June 1943.) His first collection of cartoons, *Die? I Thought I'd Laugh!*, was published in 1936 and with the approach of war he joined the Home Intelligence Department of the Ministry of Information under Mary Adams and later became deputy to Dr Stephen (later Lord) Taylor. He then moved to the Publications Division under Robert Fraser (later Sir Robert Fraser, Director-General of the Independent Televison Authority) where fellow employees included Cecil Day Lewis and Laurie Lee. Finally he moved to the Films Division where he found himself working again under his old Shell boss Jack Beddington and succeeded another former Shell colleague John Betjeman as script editor. Meanwhile, in the evenings he worked as a prison visitor in Wormwood Scrubs and (from 1938) was employed in the Auxiliary Fire Brigade based at Kensington Fire Station.

In 1939 he published a book of poems, *Second Thoughts on First Lines* and the following year came his second cartoon anthology, *Animal, Vegetable and South Kensington*. Also in 1940 he was asked to illustrate in colour the second edition of T.S. Eliot's *Old Possum's Book of Practical Cats*, which became his best known work.

After the war Bentley wrote five thrillers – *The Tongue-Tied Canary* (1948), *The Floating Dutchman* (1950), *Third Party Risk* (1953), *The Events of That Week* (1972) and *Inside Information* (1974) – and an autobiography, *A Version of the Truth* (1960), and also began a monumental Dickens index for Oxford University Press which was completed by Michael Slater and Nina Burgis after his death. Other non-fiction books by Nicolas Bentley included *Ballet-Hoo* (1937) and *The History of the Circus* (1977), and an anthology of his essays and hitherto uncollected cartoons appeared as *How Can You Bear to be Human?*, with an Introduction by Malcolm Muggeridge, in 1957.

His postwar Fleet Street work included drawing for the weekly magazine *Time & Tide* (1952-4) and the daily *News Chronicle* (1954-5). In addition he drew more than 600 daily topical pocket cartoons for the *Daily Mail* (1958-62) before resigning under the strain. He also began contributing portraits of famous people to the *Sunday Telegraph* when it began publication in March 1964 until 1971. At the age of 64 he began drawing for *Private Eye* (notably illustrating 'Auberon Waugh's Diary' from its inception in 1971 to 1976) and others.

His writing and editing work was also considerable. Having illustrated George Mikes' bestselling book *How to Be an Alien* (1946) and others for André Deutsch (then working at Allen Wingate Ltd) he became one of the three founders of André Deutsch Ltd when the publisher set up his own imprint in 1950 (the three arrows in the company's logo represent himself, Deutsch and the third founder director, Diana Athill). In addition he wrote entries on Barnett Freedman and the cartoonist

'It's for the Braemar Games – like it?'

A wartime drawing featuring Hitler and Goering, published in the
Bystander on 26 June 1940.

Nicolas Bentley c. 1947.

Bruce Bairnsfather for the *Dictionary of National Biography* and was an editor for Mitchell Beazley, Sunday Times Publications (1962-63) and Thomas Nelson (1963-67). He also edited a number of cartoon anthologies – including five volumes of *Pick of Punch*.

Though he did occasionally use colour Bentley was best known for his black-and white work which employed a fine line and solid areas of black ink in the manner of Aubrey Beardsley. Indeed, Malcolm Muggeridge in his entry on Bentley in the *Dictionary of National Biography* described him as 'a master of the thin black line' and Ruari McLean has talked of his line as being as 'even as a black thread, with no variation from thick to thin, and no shadows to counterfeit roundness; just accurate drawing based on meticulous observation' (*Nicolas Bentley Drew the Pictures*). He was greatly influenced by the work of the *New Yorker* cartoonist Ralph Barton (1891–1932) – and even dropped the 'h' in his Christian name so that his signature could appear symmetrically in two lines like Barton's. Another important influence on his style was the nineteenth-century Russian-born French cartoonist Caran D'Ache (Emmanuel Poiré) and he also admired Steinlen, Keene, Hugh Thompson, Doré, Léandre, Olaf Gulbransson of *Simplicissimus*, William Nicholson, Mervyn Peake, H.M.Bateman, the American George Price, and the poster artists Lewitt–Him. In Bentley's own words:

> It would be presumptuous of me to claim that my work bears a significant resemblance to Aubrey Beardsley's, but I am aware, for instance, that his use of heavily contrasted areas of black and white had its effect on the evolution of my own style, just as the grotesque and often outrageous exaggeration in some of Doré's humorous work affected the degree of exaggeration in my own. Again, the simplicity of Caran D'Ache's line, which can give as much individuality to the contour of a boot as it can to the posture of a figure, showed me that an economical outline may produce an effect just as telling as a detailed study.
>
> (*A Version of the Truth*, pp.126–7)

Bentley greatly enjoyed drawing nuns and priests – if only for the opportunity to use large areas of black ink – and the *Punch* historian R.G.G.Price described him as 'one of the comparatively few *Punch* artists...who has succeeded both with the humour of incongruity and the humour of social criticism'. However, he was never savage in his satires. In the words of Ruari McLean, 'He had seen the seamy, criminal and dangerous sides of life, but drew gently with the purpose of amusing – yet with devastating accuracy and sensitivity. Not many artists have done that. He can take his place without apology among the greatest of England's graphic artists.'

Elected a Fellow of the Society of Industrial Artists in 1946, Bentley was a member of the Garrick Club and one of the founder members of the British Cartoonists' Association when it was formed in 1966. Examples of his work are held in the collections of the National Portrait Gallery, the Prints and Drawings Department of the British Museum, the University of Kent's Cartoon Study Centre and elsewhere.

Near the end of his life Bentley moved out of London to a converted village school in Downhead near Shepton Mallet, Somerset. He died in the Royal United Hospital, Bath, on August 14, 1978 and was cremated in Bath Crematorium.

Mark Bryant
London, 2001

'How's about a coupla ringsides for tonight, Jack?'

The Church

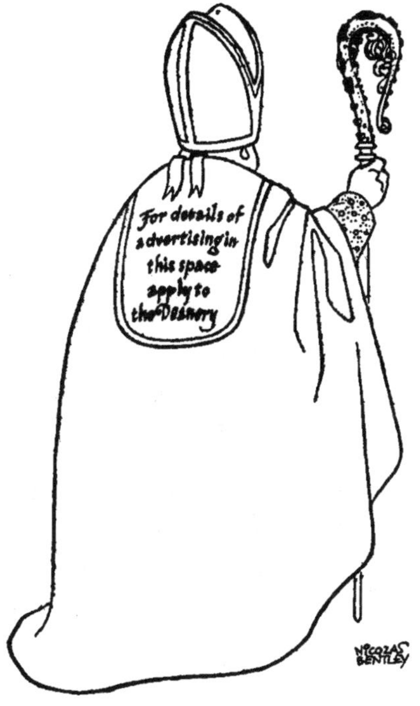
For details of
advertising in
this space
apply to
the Deanery
NICOLAS BENTLEY

'Mother Superior – and how!'

'Good Lord, we forgot the onions!'

'I ran it up from a piece I got in the sales.'

'Father, I want you to meet Mother.'

'With a hey-nonny-nonny and a hot-cha-cha!'

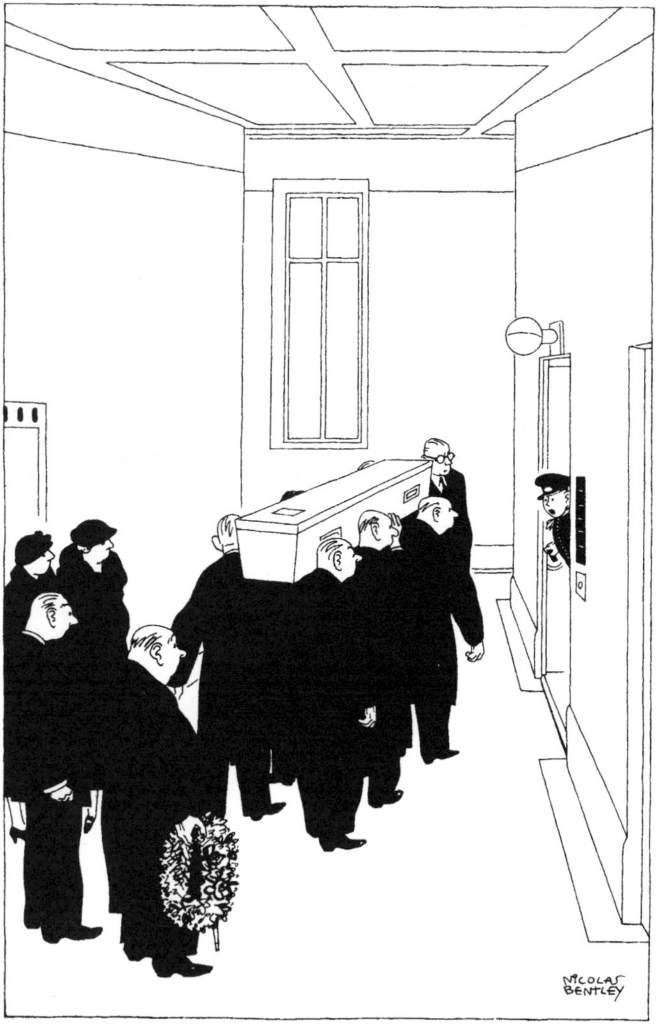
NICOLAS
BENTLEY

'Going down?'

'You've got a button undone!'

'Sergeant Murphy, I must ask you to stick to the beat.'

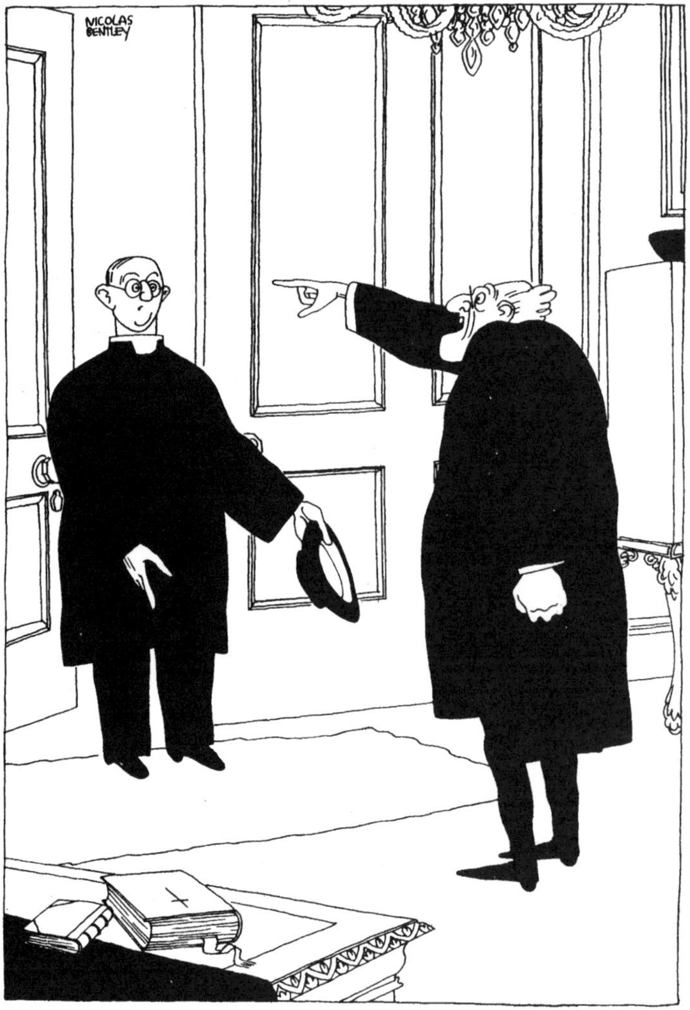
NICOLAS BENTLEY

'Canon – you're fired!'

'Come on, don't be a dog in the manger!'

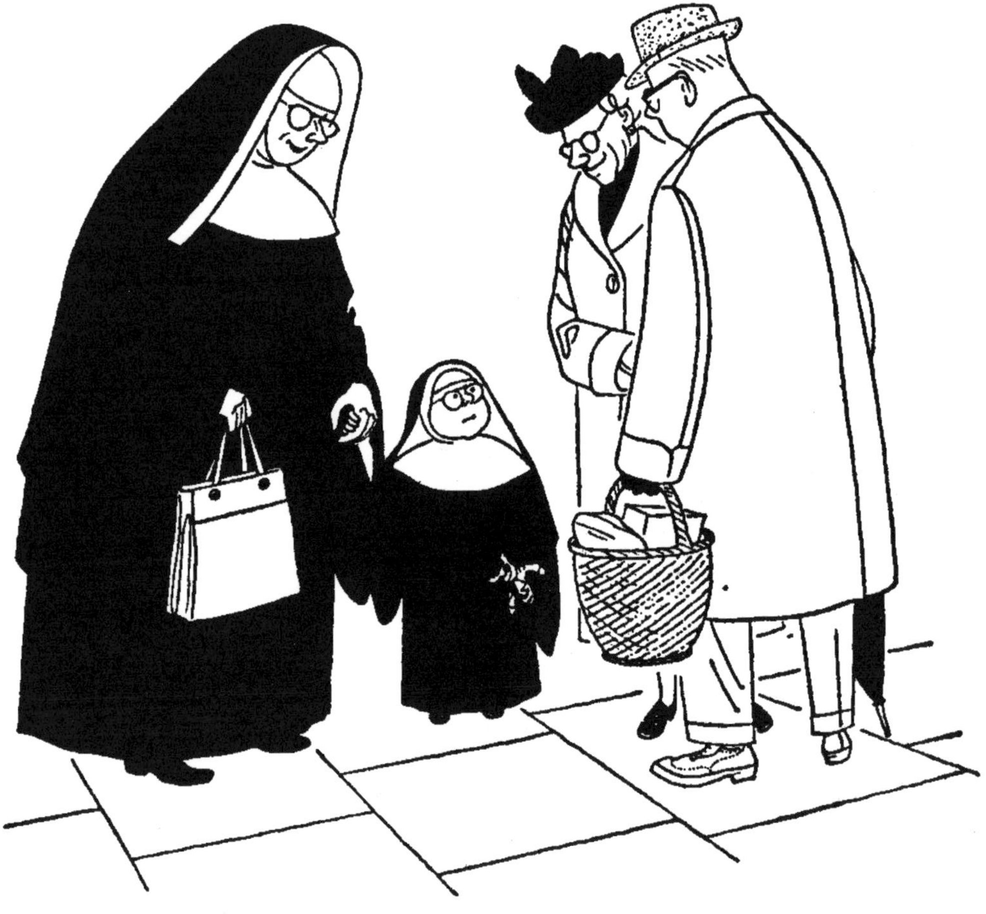

‘Say “How do you do?” ’

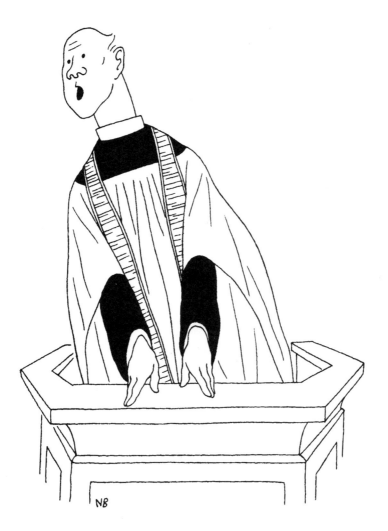

'If any of you gathered here today have heard this one,
stop me.'

'I realize that, madam, but the cost of dying has gone up too.'

'That's OK, Miss Matson, we know that's how they sing
it at the Condor Club.'

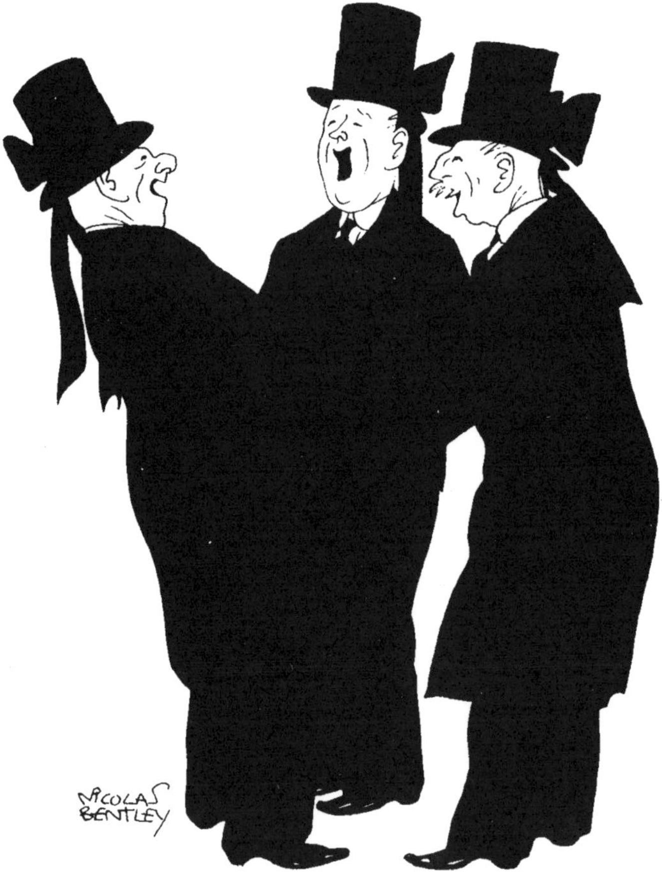
NICOLAS
BENTLEY

'Die? I thought I'd laugh!'

Flora & Fauna

'But Miss Kirkwood, it can't be a Siamese – where's the other half?'

'By Jove, William, he nearly got you today!'
'Yes, sir, 'e nearly gets me every day.'

'You won't let him worry you, will you?'

'Have I been giving it too much water, d'you think?'

'Is it part of it, or d'you think we should tell him?'

'Have you anything for a poor doggie who just *cannot* sleep!'

Now, Mr Delarue, I'm sure you're fond of pansies.'

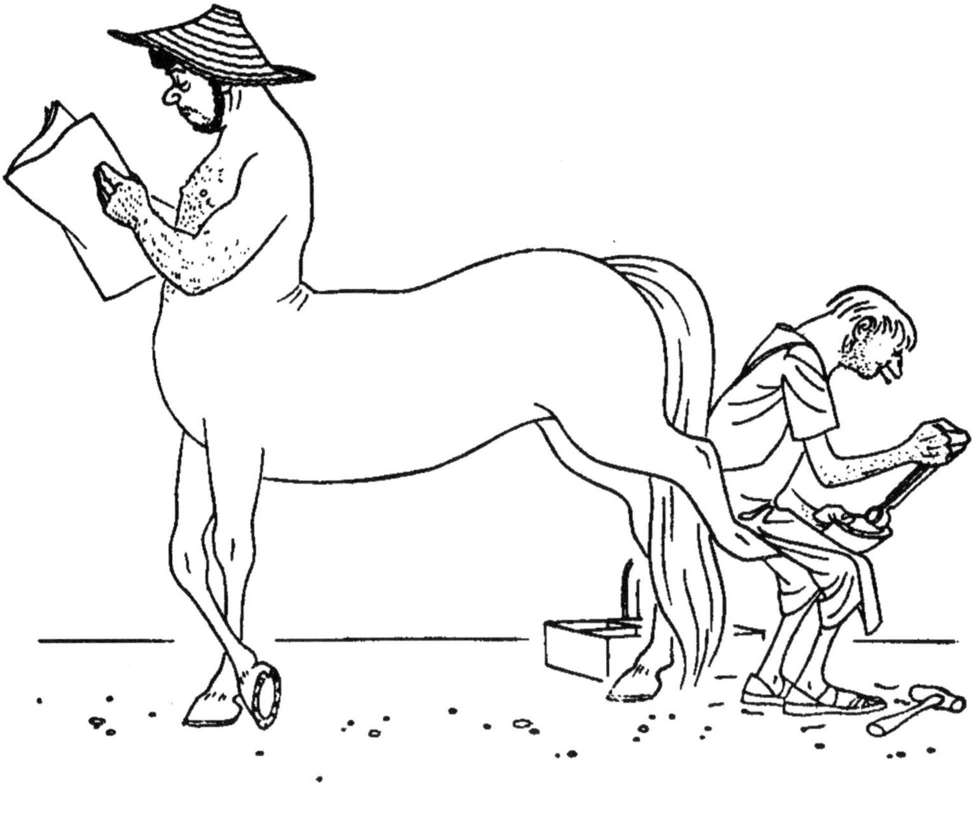

The Arts

'It's not the *real* me though, is it?'

'OK. P'raps you'd like to show us 'ow it goes yourself?'

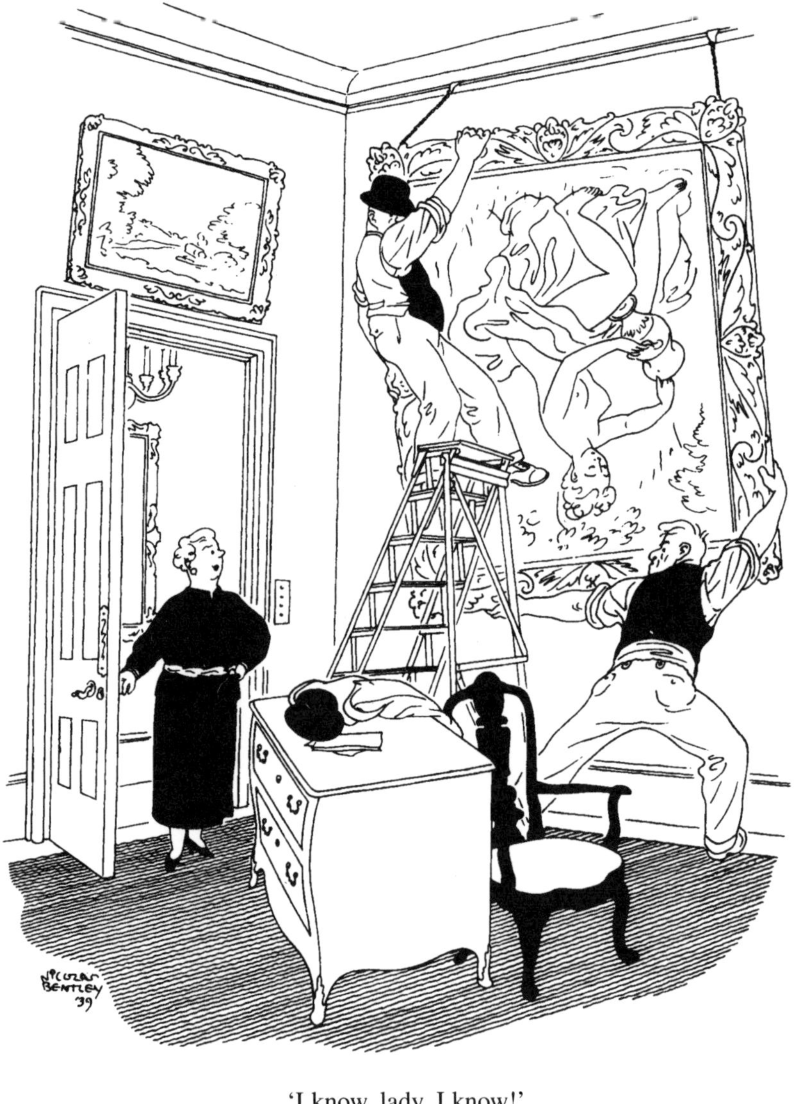
NICOLAS BENTLEY '39

'I know, lady, I know!'

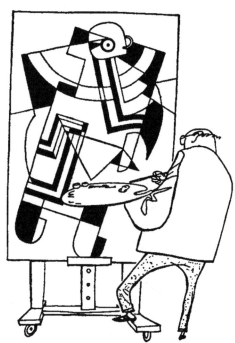

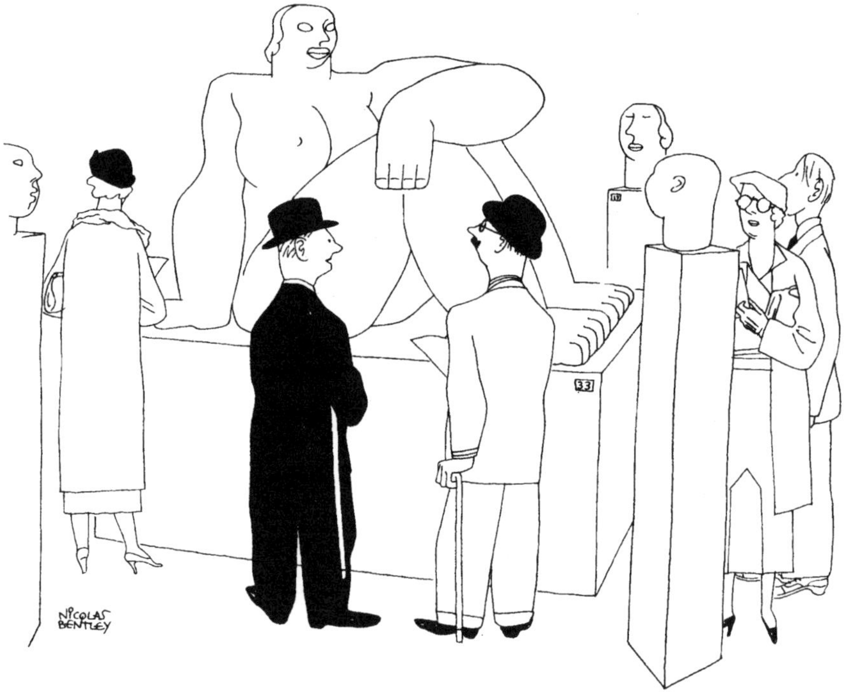
NICOLAS
BENTLEY
33

'My Aunt!'
'Not really?'

'Look – Ivy Compton-Burnett.'

'Now here's a Tintoretto, Mrs Heuffer, that'll knock your eye out!

'Are you going to Glyndebourne this year?'

'We have that on our mantelpiece.'

'Meant to be a Red Admiral, I suppose.'

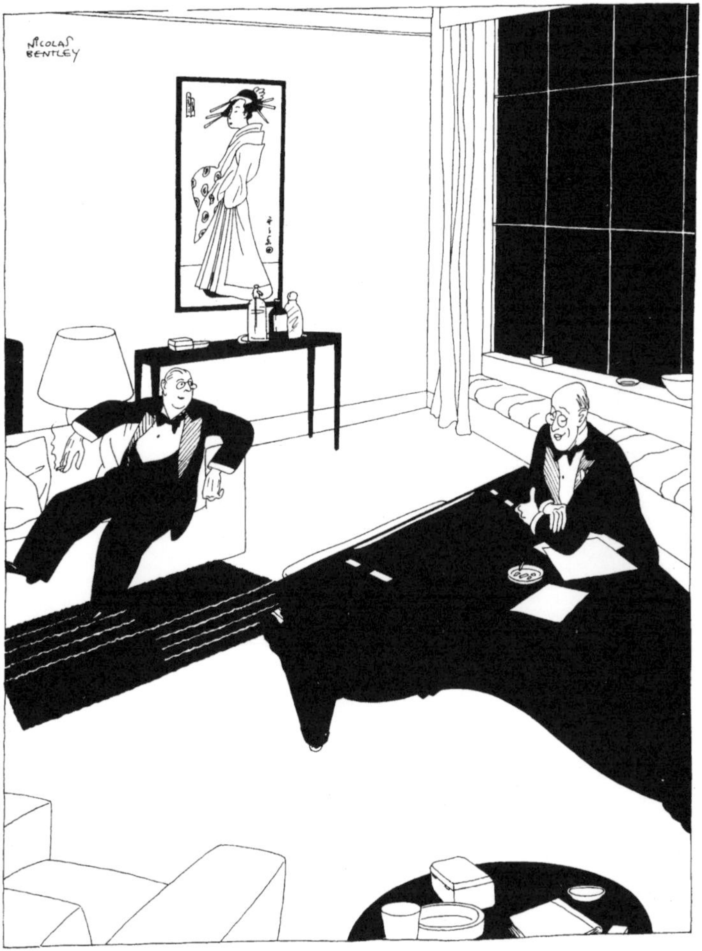
NICOLAS
BENTLEY

'Play to me, gipsy!'

'It's maddening. I cannot get a single one stolen.'

'Ooh, I do feel funny! I wish you hadn't eaten that lobster.'

'Oh, all RIGHT then, I'll buy you the Leonardo instead.'

'And I honestly wouldn't spend another winter in England,
if I were you.'

'Stap me, Sir Antony! What is this? I said I wanted a *miniature* this time.'

Going Places

'A minicab, sir? For *you*, sir?'

'I'll be sorry to part with it, but I must find some means
of paying for my season ticket.'

'This is certainly NOT a minicab, and if it were it would be
a miniature cabriolet.'

'St Pancras, please, and I should like to insure myself
as well as my luggage.'

'I always preferred the tempo on the Southern – two
hours behind time.'

Little Ones

'Listen, Dad – if I pass my eleven plus can I have a bash
at being a sex kitten?'

'I want to introduce my son.'
'What on earth for?'

'Here's Daddy, darling, run and get the screwdriver.'

'I don't mind about your maths or French literature, Julian, as
long as you get through the security check.'

'Don't tell me that's meant to be the cathedral.'

'…and this little pig went to the European Common Market and sold more agricultural machinery, light alloys and motor vehicles in eight months than it had sold in the previous year.'

'Please, sir, may I have the right to secede?'

'Am I to conclude, Maxwell, that you have suffered a bereavement
or merely that the holidays are at an end?'

'It's such a wrench when they go back to school, isn't it?'

'...while the snow lay in the upper atmosphere under insufficient barometric pressure to cause it to fall.'

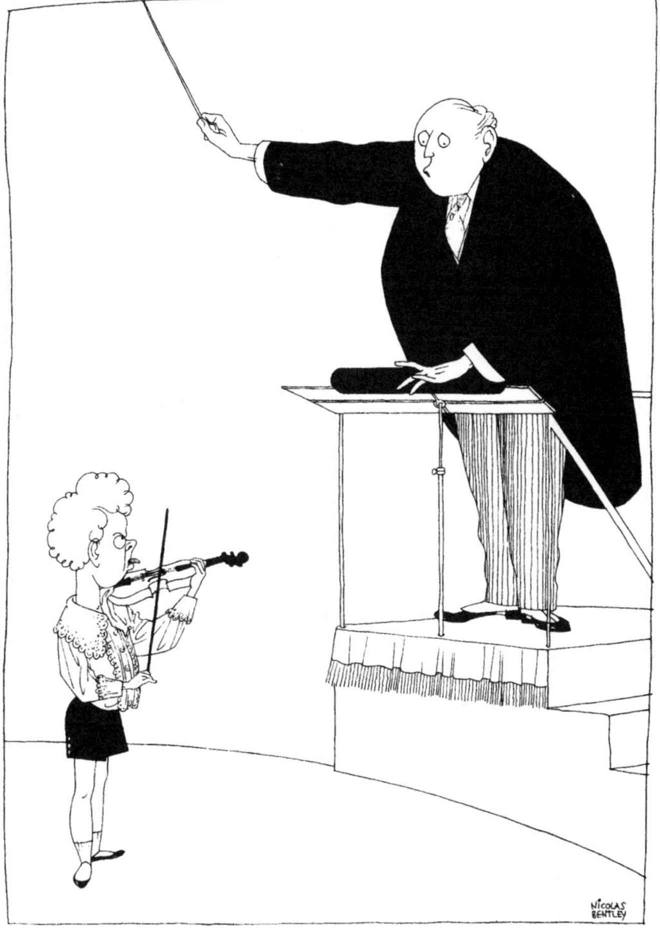
NICOLAS
BENTLEY

'*Pianissimo* yourself!'

'Dug up! You're always wanting to be dug up. Why can't you
let the child enjoy himself?'

Law & Order

'Yes, that's the man, I'm positive.'

'Come, you wouldn't wish me to use force?'

'Don't it seem silly, eh?, workin' at a bank on a Bank 'oliday.'

'Well, whatever will you rascals be up to next, eh?'

'I never thought I'd get a holiday at all this year.'

'Don't be silly, there's a credit squeeze on.'

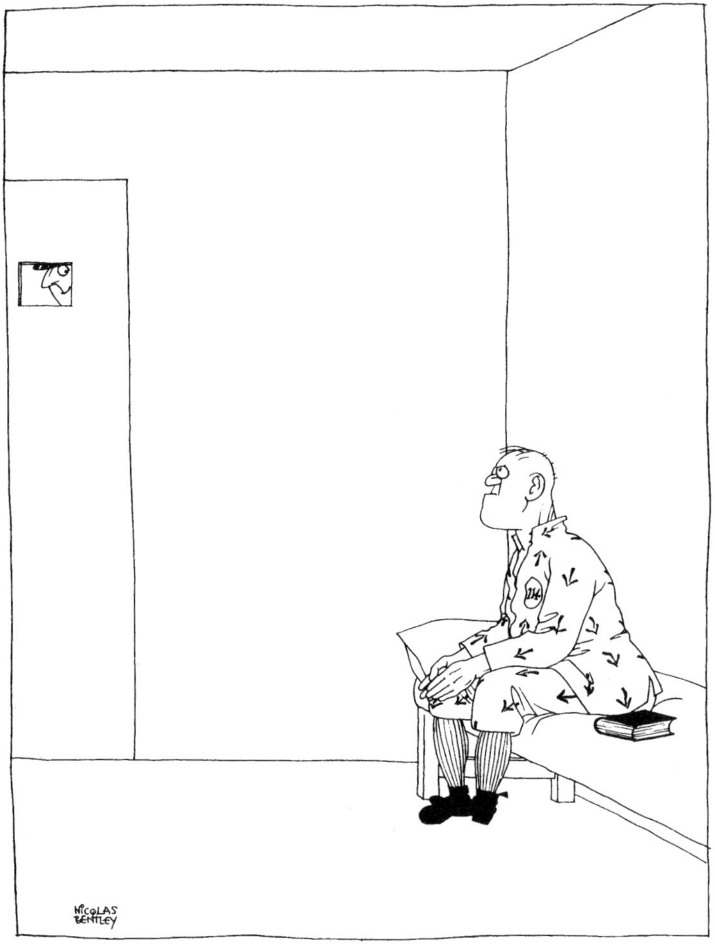
NICOLAS
BENTLEY

'Peep bo!'

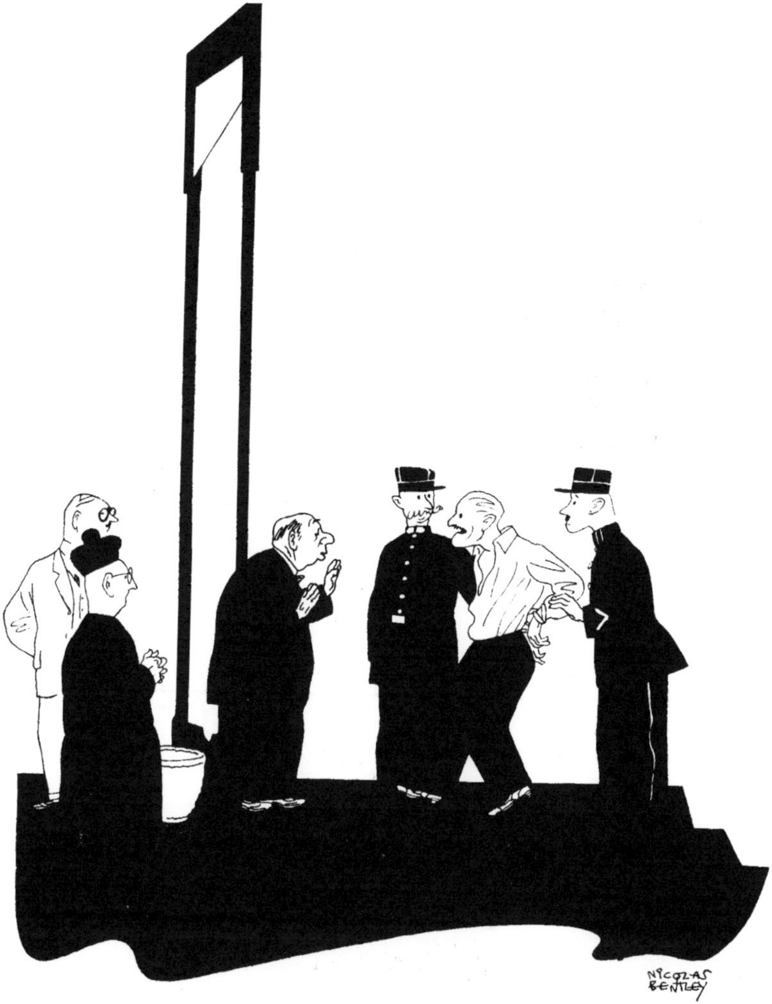
NICOLAS
BENTLEY

'Now, don't lose your head.'

'Do you plead innocent or not guilty?'

All in the
Game

'Hey! She was only meant to kick off–'

'Excuse me, what won the three-thirty?'

'I never dream of buying new lingerie till I see what
they're wearing at Wimbledon.'

'And when they've nationalized the place I suppose
the Eton Boating Song becomes the Thames Conservancy Board
and Inland Waterways anthem.'

'I wish you'd listen to me. I told you the weather was
going to improve.'

'If you couldn't stop Lavinia eloping you might at least have persuaded her to go where there was some decent salmon fishing.'

'She's been seeded Britain's No.1 spectator.'

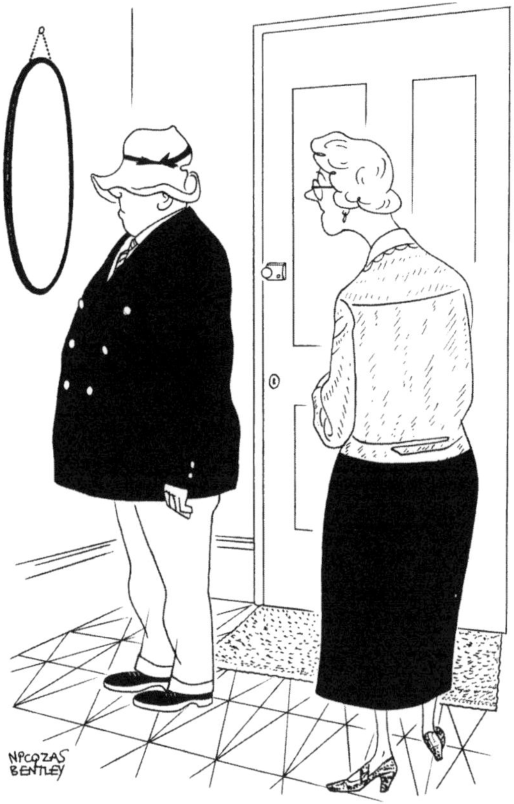
NICOLAS BENTLEY

'Don't you think it would be polite to the West Indies
if you was to get a new one?'

'You goin' to Ascot this year?'

'We've still not lost the Ashes but I should say it's tempting
Providence to put away the sackcloth.'

Political Matters

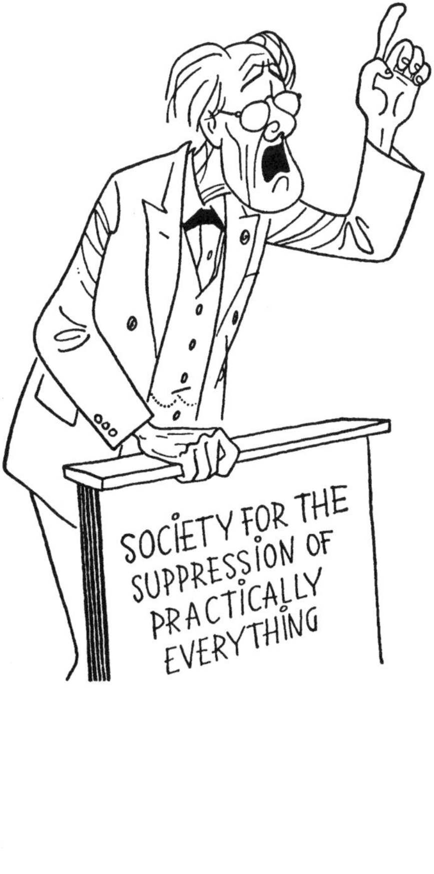
SOCIETY FOR THE
SUPPRESSION OF
PRACTICALLY
EVERYTHING

'Yes, my dear. I'm sure you could tell them how
to reform the Lords.'

'Furthermore, you can tell your editor the Watch Committee
doesn't like being watched.'

'When you said, before you got the three-line whip, that you thought the amendment was asinine, illogical and an insult to the House, it only goes to show how hopelessly wrong first impressions can be, doesn't it.'

'I don't see where you're supposed to fill in
the treble chance.'

'No, I haven't been brainwashed. I've simply reached an
intellectual decision that the PM is right.'

'Will you stop interrupting me while I'm heckling!'

'Darling, I feel absolutely terrible: I forgot today to reaffirm my
traditional faith in multilateral disarmament and collective security.'

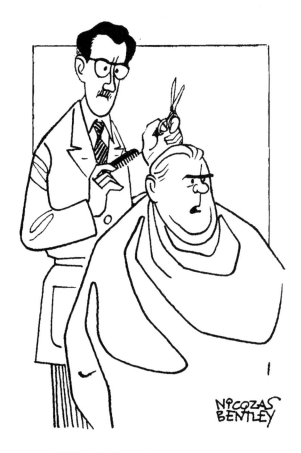

'A bit off all round, please, and no witty remarks
about the Budget.'

'Well what's the use of the national opinion poll if it isn't to find out the name of the winner?'

'By "aggressive forces of imperialism in the world arena" I
suppose he means us.'

'Would you be interested, monsieur, in a device for
stabilizing the Government?'

'If we really are going to save £90 million by cutting the
atomic programme, I don't feel I'm in a position to insist.'

'How do I indicate that to a certain extent my sympathies
are divided?'

'The Labour Party will make a fighting recovery, sir – in fact,
it's fighting already.'

'Not as good as the rock we had last year when the Conference was at Bournemouth.'

The Social Whirl

'That's my husband – over by the door.'

'Tell me, Mr Dinwiddy, how does a Scottish draper magnate
deal a counter-blow?'

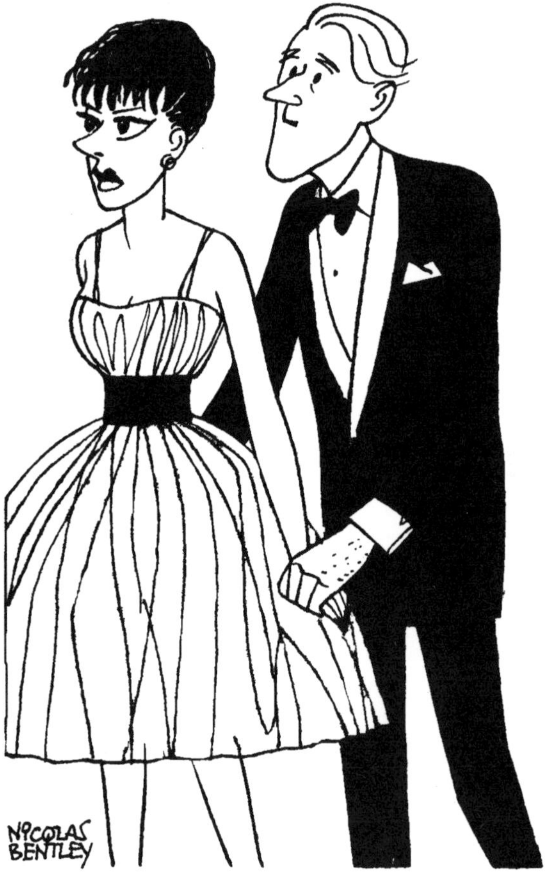
NICOLAS
BENTLEY

'But Rosemary darling, the fact that we have practically nothing in common need not stop us from making a successful merger.'

'Now what made me think you said fancy dress.'

'The Earl and Countess of Kilkenny, and no laughter, please.'

'And this, I'm afraid, is Mrs Glover.'

'Squabbling over fifty million, it seems so *sordid.*'

'She says that they've cried off the Chelsea Arts, will we meet
them at the Dorchester instead.'

'Oh Gerald, darling, at last! What made you do it? Was it
the five per cent reduction?'

'Festive greetings to you both at this season of good cheer.'

'As a matter of fact, my wife and I have always held that half her
clothing belongs to me.'

'Wonderful day at the sales, darling. I've bought all next
year's Christmas presents.'

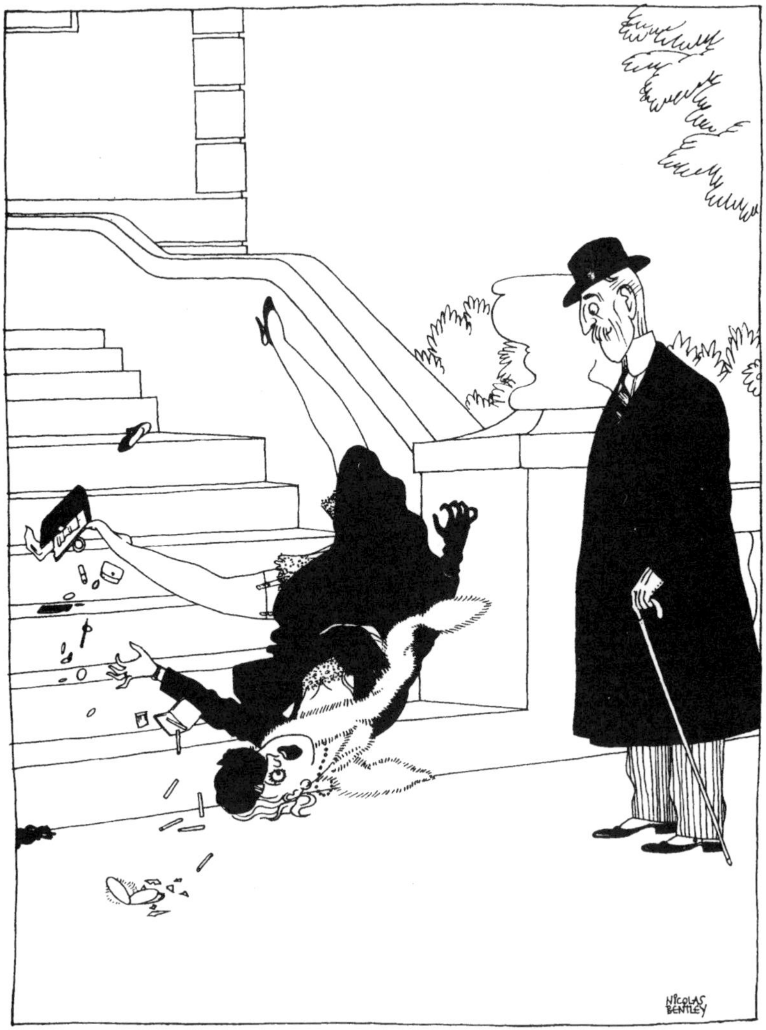
NICOLAS BENTLEY

‘Hullo – tumbled over?’

It’s a Living

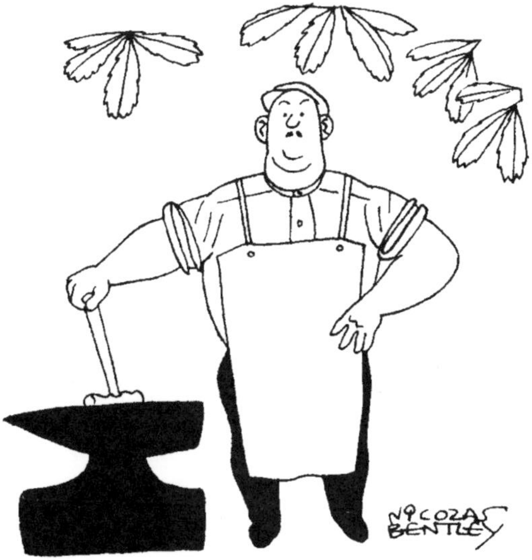
NICOLAS BENTLEY

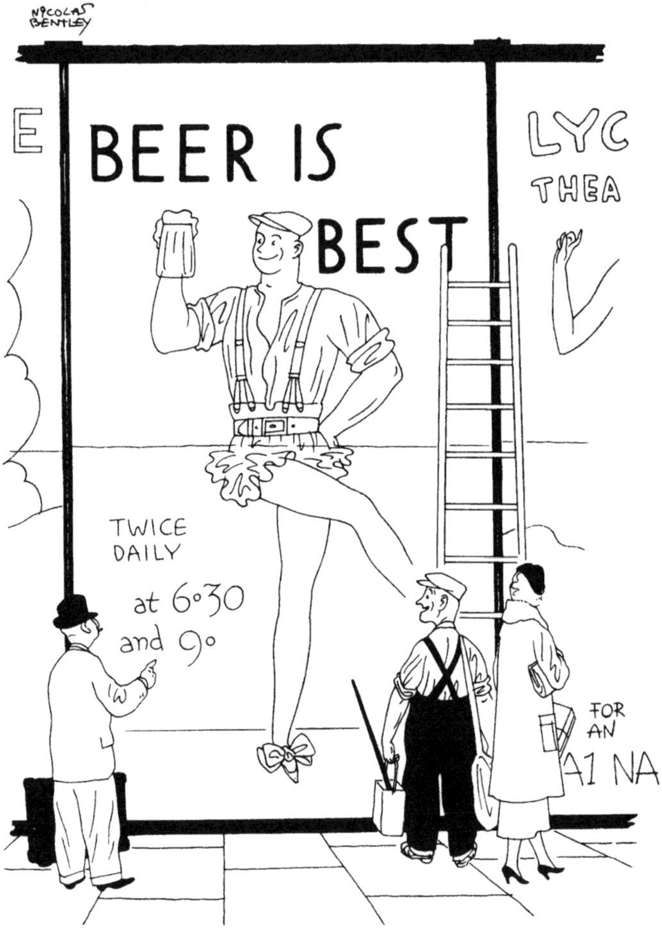
NICOLAS BENTLEY
E
BEER IS
BEST
LYC
THEA
TWICE
DAILY
at 6.30
and 9.
FOR
AN
A1 NA

‘Blimey – so I ’ave!’

'*Scusi...*'

'Did you hear that one about the square of the hypotenuse?'

'And I suppose they're actually hard at work.'

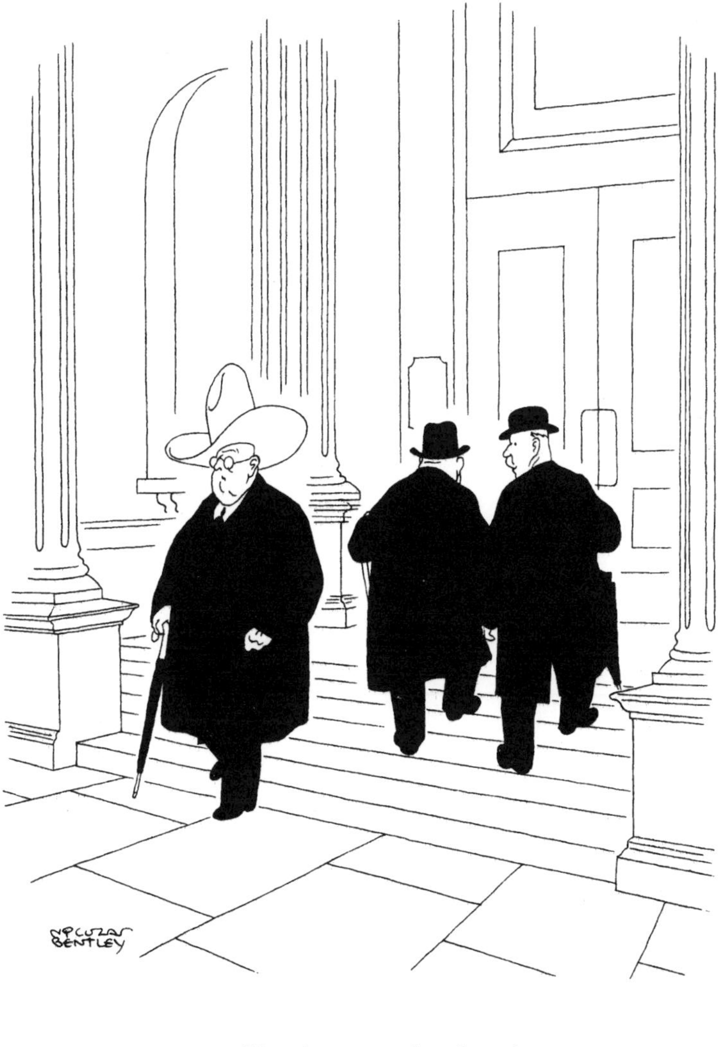

'Kerr has a new hat, I see.'

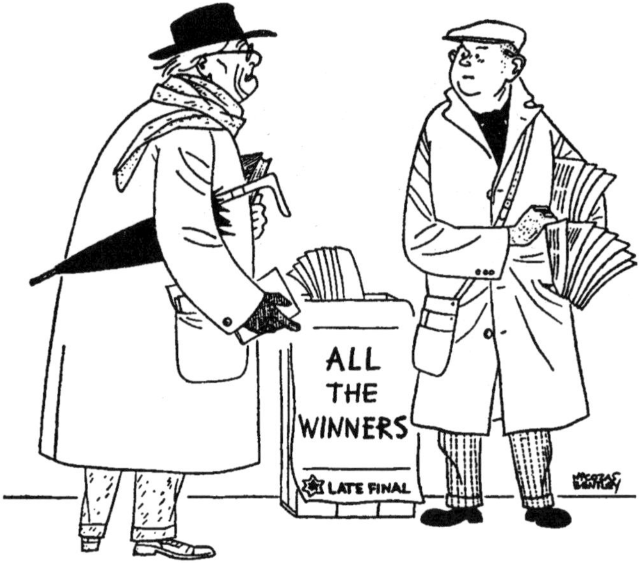
ALL
THE
WINNERS
LATE FINAL

‘Who got the Nobel Prize?’

'Get ready to run.'

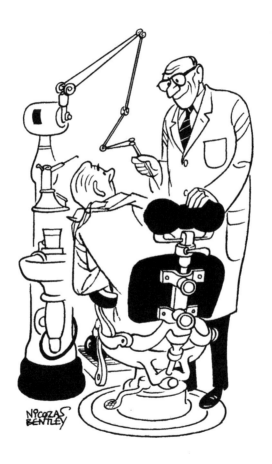

'What was it you were saying just now about the
repairs racket?'

'Smashing news, Dolly! I have to advise you that as from
the commencement of the New Year my emoluments will be
subject to increase.'

'I do so love it when autumn leaves begin to fall, don't you?'

'Shall I tell Her Ladyship you dropped in, sir?'

'Boiled cod, sir? For *you*, sir?'

Military Affairs

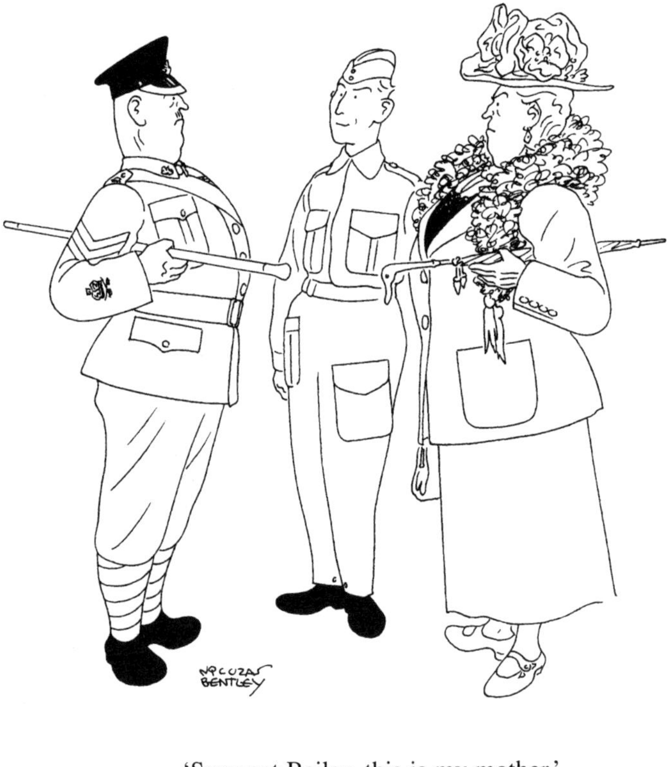
NICOLAS BENTLEY

'Sergeant Bailey, this is my mother.'

'Ah – also an Ovaltiny, I see!'

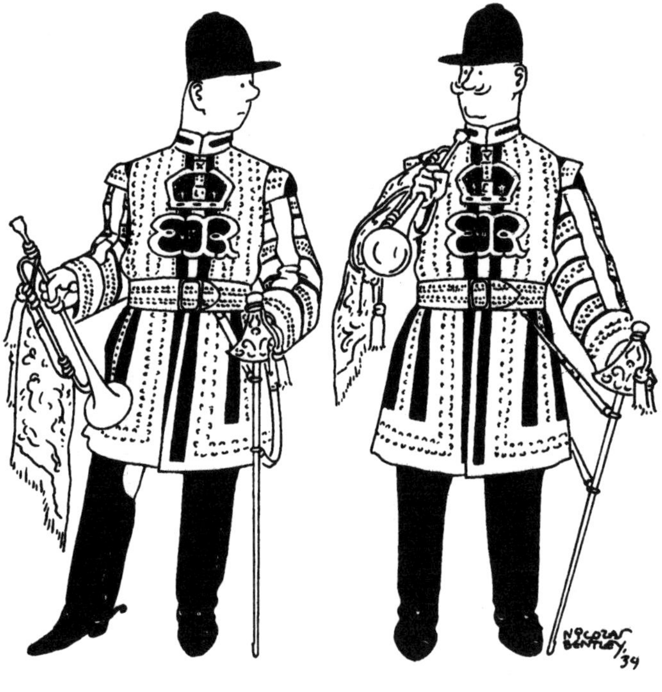
NICOLAS BENTLEY '34

'How does *Tiger Rag* go?'

'Mind, we're coming to a step.'

'Is he instead of the atom bomb, Mum, or as well as?'

Mark Bryant was born in Dorset and is a philosophy graduate of London University. After a number of years in book publishing he turned freelance, working as an editor, writer and exhibition curator. Honorary Secretary of the British Cartoonists' Association for eight years (1992–1999), he was also its Vice-President(1999–2000) and is currently Secretary of the London Press Club. He has organized cartoon exhibitions in Europe as well as Great Britain, has served on the jury of several international cartoon competitions, and has lectured on the history of cartoons in the UK and overseas. In addition, he is the author of several books – including *Dictionary of British Cartoonists and Caricaturists 1730–1980* (with S. Heneage), *Dictionary of Riddles* (Special Commendation in Best Specialist Reference Book Awards 1990), *Private Lives, World War II in Cartoons, God in Cartoons* and *Dictionary of 20th Century British Cartoonists & Caricaturists.* He has also edited/compiled more than 20 cartoon collections (amongst other books), including *The Complete Colonel Blimp, Vicky's Supermac* and *The Comic Cruikshank*, is a member of the editorial board of the *International Journal of Comic Art*, and has contributed articles on cartoonists and caricaturists to the *New Dictionary of National Biography, Encarta Encyclopedia* and *World Encyclopedia of the Press.*